Event Horizon
By Harrison Reed Gross

Event Horizon.
First edition.
Copyright 2012 Sphirah.
Printed by Createspace.
Poems written in United States 2012.
Front & back cover, Composition VII,
Wassily Kandinsky, 1913.
Author shot courtesy of Ayèlet Pearl.

ISBN-13: 978-0615710532 (Sphirah)
ISBN-10: 0615710530

As a work of art under license to Sphirah for reproduction, this product has a charitable aim, in tandem with its educational or entertainment value. This is accomplished through the special Orlah Contract, which I created as the founding principle of Sphirah to convert the positive momentum of art into a charitable force. For a maximum of the first three years a work of art is contracted to Sphirah, all of the profit it generates goes directly to the artist. After this initial period, the profit on any sale of the work is divided between the artist and any charitable causes of his or her choice. A minimum of one third of all profit on the licensed product is sent directly to the charity or charities after the Orlah Phase. The goal of Sphirah is to harmonize the artist's proliferation with his or her compassion, providing them the opportunity to raise capital for noble causes through their art.

Warm Wishes,
Harrison Reed Gross
Founder and 1st Chair Poet

A new broom sweeps clean.

...Anonymous

A selection of sixty poems...

...examining the nature of time.

Frontispiece

Time to jive to a whole new ragtime,
Palm on a polemic mélange
of ice palms frosted on
vibrating glass sublime,
I am a cherry orange
on borrowed overtime.

A kinesthetic learner,
I fumble the figure in awe.
A visual disturber,
Your iris a tearing claw.

Tongue a snake with biting rancor,
Through her, the Opponent licks me.
How far am I willing to drive this dream?
Through the past, the Opponent kicks me.

He cuts the apple into fat green slices
sated in their own devices,
and serves it like my soul on a silver pate.
It curdles my buds and dices my palate,
He laughs and I wish he'd speak about it,
But he flouts 100 vices and shouts in a 1,000 voices,

THEY WHO CROWD HIM
DOUBT HIM,
DOUBT HIM!

Poison Merchant

Bring it down to a gentle smolder,
and I'll depart a story colder than winter.

Chainsmoking on a Harlem streetcorner,
Taped-up sitar & sitarist peppering the silence.
A goodwill mission of 6,000 mangoes
Rolls casually over my toes.

All that is left is water & guilt
Waiting for sunrise on a boardwalk,
Sitting for the sun on stilts.

There's a vape taped atop the nape of the sitar,
& the sitarist drinks the vapor, his morning nectar.

An amorphous corpus in the dawn fog
coalesces with apples in its arms,
but it is bewitched fruit. A toxic bog
scrolls across devouring warmth.

The short-term is bleak,
but the future is aglow.
Like vaporous vespers fleeing,
Like melting final spring snow
Sunshine's on the boardwalk
lathering all its love below,
& the shades that stalk
cringe & balk like rabid crows.

Capacitor

IF I can resist
my existence will persist,
yet I am remiss—
Despite this,
Who could resist?

Every day I awake
I know I will sleep
closer to God.
This, or he casts me
deeper, and further
Abroad.

A slovenly samovar half-full of murky water
is all I call my own.
I *am* talking to myself,
Although I'm never alone.

I'm incurring roaming chargers,
They're after my bricks and bones.
A body hits the rivers
And is ferried to unknowns.

Balmy Breeze

Double-popped collar in the
Winterscape.
Cool hard marble bench,
Foolish friend from France,
Crusty pizza and fizzy grape.

On absolutely perfect days like this—
I can forget I am the mayor of cigarette-town,
I can forget I don't own any money cowries,
And that she will never think of me any
or evermore.

Caterwauling cardsharps and chessmistresses
eat chocolate-dipped marshmallows
and wear each other's minds
as secondhand dresses
as the second hand spirals.

Carousel

I am a loophole
In the footnote of the
Fine print in between the lines
Crafted
Gently white by the
Crescent edge of a thumbnail
Curtailed with dust under dirt
Worlds of molecular
Sabotage against
An institute of somatic
Cells
In a prison
Answering the Pavlov bell,
Wartime bells
Tolling beyond
Gates embellished
With shells.

And I spin
Again around
To where it
All started—
A twinkle in an
Eye and
A will in
A mind.

Recidivistic Pulse

Know those nights
when sunrise seems the distant past?
Yet we are minutes
from our next distant break-fast.

All passes as a cinematograph—
In the beginning I had a lemon tree
and sucked its zest with a laugh,
so even the definition of sour was a tad sweet.

Then the clock spirals ahead
a couple quick years,
past Arkansas in September
to a whole new sphere.

He came on a horse and left on an automobile.
I held her midwinter and am just arriving in Castile.
I remember New York as without that provincial feel,
And pray for my brother sinking in the high surreal.

The wick winds down another decade
and there's a blockade before every face.
An eerie glow of techno-chrome
will be your aura to the grave.

Yet slicing through this
Like a sword through mist—
An intoxicating presence
Permeates my defenses,
Skeleton watch tight in my whitened fist.

Swept away by her silk and steel,
Nothing but abandoned sushi

And tracks across a mysterious meal.
She came so nobly but adroitly seduced me.

A million one-liners later—
Another day, another diner,
Until it all blows over.
Then more insane
From more of the same.

Lovely to shiver
when you've sweat so long.
To sashay in panoramic East River
as if nothing is wrong.

From innocence I came,
and to innocence I will return.

He came for the fast and left after repast.
He came from the past and was modulated at last,
Unbuttoned his cummerbund and drove off moribund,
Into thorns of the sun.

Green looks so green against a gray sky.
I must remind, they do not die,
merely rise beyond our reach.
Singing my forelocks on bitty dyed
gunmetal box of fire box of light box of heat.

He came on a throne and left grinding millstones,
He was unknown until I brought him home.
We were both going nowhere slow.

He came a boy seeking to spend a little time,
and left a man hunting for love in his life.
But the moon is his lover tonight.

Despite my gentle coaxes, raspy thin,
And all your dizzy hoaxes so peregrine,
He became a child and was heft into a coffin.

The Problem of Evil
FOR AYÈLET PEARL

How many of my ventures
for plunder and splendor
ended in nothing
but a precious lesson?
Now I crave experience.

I want to happen upon a
Candlelit charmhouse in Carolina country,
And taste like never before.

Singer makes me feel
like grand wars are being waged,
Between
God & Evil,
Faith & Doubt,
Truth & Rage.

O Ayèlet, volcanic island,
flickering fire in my black thicket,
My pinky jammed in the jamb
Between
God's cathartic flight-plan
& Satan's pale silver serotonin screen.

The connection
between
the two?

A quaint course
on Singer's
taboo points of view.

Sad Parenting

Many a kid
is unfortunate witness
to what his parent did.

In apparent conclusions
I transparently hid,
Swathed in what
the mother did.

The overtly complex word he snickered,
Pallor creeping the veins of his wrist.
Chalkier knickerbockers bickered,
Posting ripostes hand over fist.

I thought on mine,
Never dwelling on another.
Craft in the left palm
As company clasps the other.

The quite-all-rights, caldera
beyond the percussion pistols,
Beachcomber paroxysms,
Seraph of souls
Balance the whole.

Quilt of the heavens—
You did doubt don't deny.
As penicillin on biotoxins,
His ever-alert molten eye.

The Lord beyond my shoulder,
Devil past the threshing door,
Clawing 'cross chintzy décor

to breathy greetings and shady dealings
of ash beings in a garish boudoir.

Good Morning Poetry

Good morn
poetry in the drawer,
tied with a touch of jade ribbon.

What secret,
what mysteries,
which sacral entities
Will I wade into the dawn berries?

There is my spirit
in the vibrating glass.
You notice a dream in the little quakes,
the way ospreys take flight when Earth shakes.

You swear a vow
not quite knowing how
or where you will be free...

Ornithologist & the Afternoon

Rabid doves
Sugary ravens,
Ceramic owl,
Malta by avian.

A flight to nowhere
cloud-scared

The white-blue-green
of a mollifying daydream,
No blackened chicken nightmares,
No rattles beyond the screen of
the coop,
the aerie,
the nest,
Just a rest for your wind-weary wings,
your ruby eye and tawny talon clawing,
Straddling the heart, chest and hair.

It's hard out there
for a
dove.

Pigeons and paraffin lamps
are perusing periodicals
and pericopae through monocles

with crumbs and dew
in lunchpails.

A Falconer for a Friend

Hey there, amethyst sky,
Could it get worse, could it?
Oh, do not tempt the Lord,
You could always inadvertently make it worse.

However, things could always get better,
A squab flutters onto the butter
Yet another blasts a fecal storm—
No calm, warning, shape or form,
Just a feather and mutter right out the door.

Howdy friend of another feather,
Today I received a long letter
Deliberating the adventures
Of my windlost brother.

Crop milk in her crop,
Air in her cere?
She sears me in tar and hair.

I have a warm, languid wish
To meet his ventures with a halfstep,
Perhaps somewhere in the Alberta auroras,
Or on the belly thermals of a magic lungfish.

Formica Fjord

Comprehend coronated chrysanthemums.
Conceive big plastic bags of fresh, fat
mango slices streetwise.

Teeth like a flock of ooze
as the first issue of your womb.
Blue boy in a grass hat.

Lens behind a 2-way mirror.
Linguistic framework dissects reality
to gaslight green and Daybreak in C.

I knew it would grind down to tonight
at the track,
Down to my last Dunhill
at last call.

Crinkled Paper Fortune Teller

Old croaking oracle—
Teeth of gold
Eyes like bone.

Her tent is gilded
with cool caramel complexions
and sharp spearmint smoke.

Her tranquil lies
a digital baroque

She draws a future
in wax and sand.
She scrapes both *drachmae*
from my sweaty hand.

Suddenly somehow she is sure
in plaintext
in pure sex on the horizon.

She screams
as she looks
at me—
ANTHROPODERMIC BIBLIOPEGY
(I will be buried in my books.)

As I left she spat a final bit at my ear,
Don't waste your money on fancy muffins and shit!

Wait a minute…
how did she know I hit the bakery
every day this year?

Footprints in Cinders

Intrigue in charcoal
On the village corkboard.
Not a dare, not a care,
For I lived there no more.

I was just passing through,
A westerly wind,
Coming to wrest a rest
From my old townsmen.

A dybbuk in the wood!
The kiosk claimed.
Fifty cowries for his blood,
Tsale is his name.

I knew that wood
And drew my hood,
As this was not good.
Damn, I thought, just my bloody luck.
Who alone could slay the dybbuk?

A bite from a rice cake
And a puff from my pipe...
I set off beyond the oxbow lake
Into the torch-lit night.

In this life
You have pioneers
And marineers,
All else a little disjunction
Between their sneers and beers
And tears.

Being both,
As a hardy lot of sand and sea
Had come unto me,
I strove the mangrove coast.

Soon out *Tsale* burst—
Much too much for me.
He did me in in the way worst,
He stole my pride first.

Moonlit Musings
CONCERNING OLSON'S SUN

Moon,
Where are you tonight?
The way is dark,
I am without light.

Lace
Lacy light
On sallow skin.
Where are you tonight?
I miss your lights again,
And the polarized prisms
Refracted off your skin.

Moon,
Akin to kin,
Friend of all dim doing.
Bent on entering my dim prison.
Sluice of bluish-white blooming.

Plumes of milky
Blood
Drip into moon-
lit mud. Alone
in the mossdeep drossy
moonless loam.

Moon,
Fabled compatriot
Of bards and wax-winged lovers,
Shine your cream complexion
Aback our festooned benediction,
On doves and owls of the bowers.

Cat & dove
In the alley,
Pitch & fear.
Then peeks in the ally
of nighttime
dire & dear.

Moon
at last in my wooden room.
I can roam the wood
for its pearly plumes.

Lunar Oars
CONCERNING TURNER'S FISHERMEN AT SEA

Moon-cold alone,
Only boat glow
in a wide radius island
of our foam isolation.

You with the paraffin—
Caveat.

Our lifeline is nil,
A wish, a wick,
A partner's ill.

I wist it where you were,
Like the sky painter's bill—
Black never flushing bluer,
Moon a cruel, light drill.

The Dark

It drains the soul,
Consumes the spirit,
And kills the crickets
That in time should near it.

The wailing poet
goes to towns below,
The towns that will not hear it.
Wails instead to the roosting crows
Waiting for God or Godot,
Who ever know not to fear it.

It fills the holes,
It eats the harlot,
And passes by the dying crickets,
from the towns, in cold parlor shows…
The sunlight will never near it.

Twilight fades
The masquerades.
The poet sits in the shade,
The shade sits upon the poet
in the towns that will never know it.

The blacking glades fade blacker still,
Where the flutist plays his trifle trill.

We play our roles
Unscripted, as we see it,
And shovel coal
Into the furnace searing
The great furnace that sears our souls,
Which in time would near it.

Moonlight lays black as coals
Yet we ever know not to fear it.

In the clouds
thunder blows,
While in the towns
Darkness rolls,
Down below the furnace cheers
For it is feasting on our fear,
And in the cotton bolls
Sleeps the weepy poet
For he will never know it.

Crying is the glowing soul,
Lying on the moonlit shoal.
The pauper and the king are coal
Shoveled in the furnace.
And unlikely flit the singing crickets
To the lasting streaks of spirit
That ever know not to fear it.

Will-o'-the-wisp

I rose from my body
as the petals of an ethereal rose.
My hem snagged on a dented diadem
Alongside my sweet corpus' repose
Gaudy Death chews a green stem.

Whisked to a twinkling grove little wooden enclave,
But am I alive? Or justly dreamily waiting to graze
in Nirvana, leagues from here?

A brown recluse skitters from dust web stasis,
with him his liquefactive necrosis
like a *shuriken* to the shoulder.
I spat a grim yodel and shuddered over.

Angel of hegemony gulfstreams me back in
A dream above you, sweet corpus, life lava skin,
Hem me in again, dented diadem.

White Water Rafting

White water rafting,
White water rafting...
Cascaded,
Rocked.
Brown Bread.

Well,
Device of fantasy,
Which will it be—
The high road,
Or the low?

I must say I am a slave
for drast and rad change.

Dirty frequency baby,
Blaster worm in my mainframe.
Steampowered amplification
and not nearly enough gain.

Your speaker got a trojan virus.
Now we have no music.

The cheshire in the
chestnuts cackles with glee,
Then purrs insidiously.

I'm so very far from my dojo.
ꝏ
Vision. Finance. Recruitment.

Realization.

I sip a walnut chalice
with a hint of malice, there is
Golden light in my palace.

How vapid.
I can hear one
Skritching at the
Trapdoor,
Luckily my room holds
A hidden corridor.

∞

What's a couple weeks,
When eternity lies ahead?
Yet each minute without you
is a slow tick.

What if death is only the beginning?
Adventure awaits,
On an endless stair of infinite days.

Redirect
Tellurian time
To heavenly ideals.

I fill my heaven with airships and gear,
And that's the top trinket I've inked all year.

Frayed Fireworks

I am a toucan opera singer
Living next to an awful singer.

Annoy,
Molted by your blather,
Clean-swept by an
Alloy alleysweeper
and a cobalt cowcatcher.

Is it softcore twilight propaganda?
Is it a hazy idea of psychic effects?
Are there invisible forces
that exert their authority
in unseen ways?

Small cloth large.
Meet someone new.
Good girl dirty.

She lives in a triangle,
Likes to be the girl in a glass box.

I'm allergic to my birthmonth
As ladies of a large vocabulary.
A night where you could be
Shattered like a snowglobe.

What geist would,
What ice could
Freeze a ghost wolf
In its wispy venom tracks?

A park is a werewolf.

Morningside Park is the werewolf broodmother.

Is a heartbeat so asunder a hoofbeat?

Is bardsong so different from birdsong?

ᏊᏊ

9 o' clock coming down
like a razor.

My pathology is a fine white
like grains of rice.

Bad management and no direction.
De-lump throat.
No signal.
Dead on arrival.

Thundering past
Fungus in your lungs,
My wheels all cough, hiccup and burp,
and if I'm lucky a lurch.

Silence is nice.
Interleaved individuals
Entangled with the intangible,
Is there greatness
Without madness?

You can't sleep in a pipe dream.

Do come on,
I can see the bright flames beyond.

ᏊᏊ

My fraternity is all sex, slaves & heroin
at the bottom of the 9th.

I'd never faced elation
Until seedcake in a space station.

I spilled bleach on hands and hair
Because of the splotch of yogurt I got on Mirage
Chair,
my illusory throne.

A playset of black cats napping on
The parameters of a navy sofa.

A varicolored fire burns within us all.

Fashion:
Pink, green & teal words,
A rabbi in a purple shirt.
Yellow fedora meets black beret,
Silk stirred down to the bustier.

Thanks for reminding me
of resplendent machines—

Saunas,
Aloe jacuzzi,
Sensory deprivation chamber.
Load me into the magazine.

I paid in time, money and memory.

Have a Cincinnati.
Twist-off crown.
Snap this girl into a woman
like a twig.

...Or nod, grin,
Sip, swig?

Been a cruel morning,
Off to a rough start,
Knocked my venus flytrap
All over my art.

Wing & fang
Lightning in a bottle.
Bat in the attic.
Feed it through the saw.

Signs pointing North,
Rivers bounding South,
And far more ice-drifts
than ought be allowed.

Pay dirt. The genizah!
Mind as an afterburner,
Eyes like sunken treasure.

Where Superb Starlings
And Japanese Waxwings reside,
I slip unmentionables down a bronzed backside.

Let me share and spurn my fear,
Air lips, I am 20 in poet years.

Arrive at prominence,
Be brought to bear.
Your turn.

Acrylic Ribbons

A little bit of hip
came sashaying down the way,
Greeting my daybreak
with a streak of azure.

There I am,
Fate bearing down 2nd Avenue,
Moments late and well-to-do.

I wonder where she is,
Grace traipsing up 76th—
A peppermint twist,
A licorice kick
Gnawing on a cinnamon stick.

ထ

An egg hatches into a bicycle.

Things are not what they are,
Nor what they seem to be.
We are swanly dreams
pillowing out the chimney.

ထ

Foam is a
loamy cobra,
Twin spiders in the soap.

Unduly domineering darksome devouring?
Or illuminate all of the senses
On bulwarks of fireworks
Bursting in every dimension.

A little something surreal
Came shifting up my scene,

I was a mellow blue
But the signal was green.

Don't think I can ever do that again—
Sit on some May hems in summer mayhem.

A Jar of Honeyed Lemon
FOR IZZY HOWELL

I like your shadow,
Izzy Howell.

Dawn is brief,
But the way well-travelled.

I had a drizzly belief
in statuesque blonde dogs,

And now just one leaf will do
in this bog of bubble & fog.

Clock of Portents

Write my name in the sand
To foretell my coming.
I will rustle through the brush,
Pressing aside a vine lattice—
Whimbrels of paradise alight on a waterfall,
Smooth, cerulean, and lush.

The jungle is a maze
Of perilous forays—
I whet my machete on stone.
And resume, into knee-deep underbrush,
Bowers above woven, wet, as if glass-blown.
Toward its core, raspberries crush.

So as I understand—
You are cross-legged in a clearing
Leering into the trees,
Pining for none other than me.
Anointed with a holy oil,
keen as a serpentine coil.

How lonely are the signals,
The light, misted drizzle—
The abyssal night so dismal.
How lovely are the omens,
Foreseen, soft-feathered, cascading—
Secured by one's leaden threads,
slight and fading.

The Fly Bartap

Say it's our last day,
Shall we take the scenic way?
And muster much milieu about you,
mildewy dew in my trebuchet.

Ghost town leaves swirl as around
a majestic pillar of gravity.
Transient babbling Ladinu in Morningside Park
a prickly sonic assailant of my smooth dark.

Night spreads like black butter,
a still heart is wont to flutter.
A stilled wing, bound like no other,
In sly dreads of night, the psychic gutter.

The resident enigma peddles darling demonologies,
her slim cigaret an angry meteor.
Frozen and quickened in blonde bronze frieze,
the past meted out the doggy door.

The fly bartap clapped the bar he tapped
a couple o' bubbly couple o' bubbly
Swirling elixirs,
Fixed her a couple o' bubbly
Swirling elixirs,
Mixed her a hookah to boot,
as for me, scotch no mixer.
They 86'd her with the unslick tricksters,
and all I had was her floozy acid on my suit.

Witness Protection

I'm changing my name to Avigdor
and moving to Scandinavia.

From there I will be Tadashi,
a fisherman in Osaka.

Frontiers attract like a magnet.
I long for sunset expanses
of grain dying garnet.

Meanwhile in Hokkaido,
I hike the foamy north slopes.

Then salty air and sea
crash against my rowboat.
I float the strait to the Canaries,
A bright star my only hope.

I'm going to the Galapagos,
where the world grows seas from my woes.

Hymn of the Tides

Through the days the tide ebbs and flows,
While my mind weeps in mighty droves,
Until I reach the sounding sea—
Where I am wakened,
Where I am free.

Out flowed the beauty captured in twists,
Manifested emotion from a fleeting mist.
I coiled a little piece of my soul
and drowned it in a dry bottle,
And prayed it remained whole.

I etched my epitaph on the back of my hand,
While a distance away fishermen in yellow rubbers
Scowled and pointed, bargaining in the sand.
Unshaven and rotten, with boorish brothers
Forsaken by peace, forgotten by lovers.

When it dwindles and when it surges,
When it storms and when it soothes,
When it salves and when it scourges,
When it's coarse and when it's smooth
is when I prevail, and when I lose.

Triangle Night

I linger alone after nightfall,
And soft like stone I press against pillows.
Swilling from empty glass bottles
Stacked discordantly on the brink
Of mottled, peeling walls.

I wipe the crumbs off my cheekbone
From the inverted chip bag above my face,
And eat huskless rice from sopping paper boxes—
In a daze I switch on the television toxins

Oh what fools these mortals be!
Sharply speaks the Shakespeare reenactment.
Forthwith resentful derision I pick a pen
And make an incision upon my skin-surface.

Well, the quicker I can down liquor
The faster I can be your master
And snicker delighted at pale alabaster.
What would they say?
Frowning rabbis and pastors.

It is quixotic, erotic, neurotic—
Automatic, didactic, daedal and dreadful
sinful, plentiful, curious, and hurried
the worried world that I must end,
distended and rent

Salted sun of my planet, like a brown carnival pretzel
Plush, crusty, cooked, twined, crooked snake
Bizarre in all your majesty, holy extoller
I linger alone until daybreak.

Hallowed

Everywhere I gaze upon
I see wingless angels and withered palms.

And as this planet's moons
cast their beams upon my neck,

I flicker out of reality's tunes
to assemble my soul from the wreck.

Signs to Jerusalem

Bust out of that bad rhythm,
Let it take you.
This is God's beach.

Flower grows out of the barrel of a gun.

Tallow & dandelion on the mantle
drip down in prides onto my sandal.

ᴆᴆ

Woe be me—
Unshelled, with a bunch of theory.

True, she was with me, befuddled,
As I analyzed the parameters of the puzzle,
We popped into pomegranate promenades
of promiscuous promise
Where she will squeeze your hand
And nudge your knee,
Perhaps bless you with a kiss.

Fire & water
Mixing on the shores of
Clearwater.
The waves skate forth,
and skitter back to their Master.

Amazed, amused and fazed
On the slaloms of love,
In the sedge mazes thereof,
Its bright blissful redress—
To coalesce in our next caress.

72 degrees

and a bit of breeze,
Praying on the dream aspect
and capacity.

∞

This fish is far from fin—
Too soon to grin, too soon to grin,
My love's wound round the cotton gin.

Too soon to sin monsoons of sin,
My love's locked in the cotton gin.

Two loony bins and a boon to win,
And my love waltzed out the cotton gin.

But nothing at all, shadows on the wall.
She does not walk back to me when free.
Hunting for brilliance,
Lost in flinty fields.

Well, nothing like a long, uphill hike
to start your morning right.
Seagulls in a gusty gully
are upright and radiant,
Like banners in wartime.

It was like discovering it for the first time,
the true gradient domineering life.

Like a haven for the clean,
A Rubicon of lava,
Like nausea seafoam green.

We roll and fold like lordly laundry,
Then hewn to road hues
where comets and cornets

blast ahead and in the rearview,

As firefly nets
Freezing fear and loss
to cindering beards of moss,

And the transfinite China syndrome
Can only yield a new dawn, a new home.

Signs to Sheol

Don't be misguided by my casual attire.
I assure you I am quite serious,
Like nighttime,
Like fresh-baked rolls from heaven.
So sizzle in this resin,
Unleavened knight in white.

Learn something about a way
of life far from your own,
And your yore
could tell us more.

Clocks fly
swiftly when high.
And I would learn something
when I tried to earn a farthing,
and ended as ashes
in an ern-carved urn.

The mark was of a minnow,
a nothing, a whoreson,
in a riverside house
in Hastings-on-Hudson.

I cut down the door with a diamond saw.
I wanted to be quick and angry, crazily raw.

No fretting.
The essence was time.
The target acquired,
already mine,
for I once grew tired
in the House of Windy Pines.

I'd seen the gem before,
In a curio cabinet in the corner.
But when I reached to restore,
Action from the rear saw me to the floor.

A moment too late,
My spirit was slaked.
Fiery furies vanished
as Yah became apparent.

It began with ego death—
No longer a mantis ronin,
But in the tapestry,
Sewn in.

I rose from a crack
in the splintered kraken house.
Rose with no teeth,
No north & south.

I spun toppling in the divine blast—
The Lord on His loom
weaves timespace into the past.
When His fingers feel our threads,
We are present, pheasant & asp.

God is that moment before now,
When they've robbed you blind,
Right to the poorhouse.

He swirls the clouds with His finger.
The earth swallows His anger.

You could die

and the moon
will still be round and bright.

I want to feel the it in my hand,
As clay in my palms,
Castles of sand.

He holds the world in a crucible,
and fiddles our fates in one sweet decibel.
The morning is upon His anvil.
He hammers out our malleable minds.

He whirled the world,
My tail curled.

Every bird, word, verve and nerve—
He taps Earth like soft serve,
slowly, sweetly,
from a profitable, gleaming machine.

But times I am knackered by clack
In blood drying black,
I am my best,
At my apex,
When I am dirty with the world.

Lighthouse in a Blackout

I was lost
but have found the way,
A wizard of peace,
Spade in the clay.

The days are getting a
dash more dyslexic,
Deeper
in the camber of this vortex.

Splay open
your palette
and speak.

Let's play pool and shoot
some color across the room.

Pick up your crayon, baby,
we'll make it. Maybe.

Achieve. Behold. Results.
Be brought into the fold
of juicy inspiration.

The mind is a frontier
that swells with every breath.

Why can't a poem be a painting?

Why not a man with wings?

At the end of the day,
the sentence will capture it.

A sentence is a camera,
and I center you in my lens.

This is my poetry,
To rhyme a picture with a sound—
To rise in cubist madness
and sink in the sweet surround.

Maple can wait.
Bad volume can wait.
Space, down clutch can wait.
Flowing loaded glowy purple overcoat can wait.

I am the rocket fueling this castle,
Quicksand is the name of my band.
I lost the way
but have found the map
of ambigrams lovely in my hand.

My dove laid an egg today!
In a week,
a squab will hatch.

Can't have white without black,
Heat without cold,
as my pastels melt out
in the snowy air.
Black brings white to bear.

Time is the cherriest dimension.
Sense, the 5th, emotion, the 6th,
thought, the 7th, and will, the late 8th,
are not worth a wit of mention.

We have lost the way
and have no map, not one.
The iniquities of the father
are visited upon the son.

With a sigh,
with eyes that ply and apply,
True leadership will always be in short supply.

Heaven forefend languid temptations
of entheogens and empty oceans,
Maybe you will buy a further confection,
A frittered conviction,
A firmer direction of fervent fiction,
And a shaded lectern of Jew skin.

You can build an empire,
but you'll need gold.
You can live forever
on a shard of soul.

Today I read a newspaper
and felt the pleasure of the past
in vain.

Sit falsely and salt your soup,
Watch time splinter by on the poplar.
Dazed by 4,000 years of news,
Just to see nothing has changed.

Girl, do you know of ancestral power?
Time scores the roots of the poplar,
tore out Port Royal from its foundation.

Tighten your fist,
influence the prince,
give the sign for the death penalty.

Brush the crumbs from your sleeve,
this soup is a bit too salty.
His diet is fried saltines
of yesterday grief.

The age of jazz has usurped the age of the waltz.

I left justify my hair
and head to the chocolatier.

Ponder the sea,
Don't harm a flea,
Sing to me from your Bodhi tree.

Alternate *sotipanna*,
Is it safe to cross?
Will I always have my
Heschl's gyri?
If You can assure no down time between,
I am the poet of this dirty slow glassine dream,
so start that purring limousine.

But don't go without a map,
You could get lost. I was lost
but have found the map. I lost
the map and am lost again.
Yet have I really looked for it,
in all this garbage I don't need?
Where is the road?
Where is that word?

To where am I going,
The world is already here.

I remember my heart is a map,
And my mind a mapmaker.
So it will be stars by the lantern,
Heart and mind by day,
I was lost but have found the way.

Darkroom in a Surge

I know you want to change the world,
but bring your thinking to a local scale.
What are we going to eat tonight?
You're looking awful pale.

Eclipse of lips,
Fly by night,
Load into the ghost of the machine

Via cable car, gravity rail, skylight or ski-lift.

So this is the meaning of down,
Down, down
through lakes and lairs
with an awl through my ear.

ᗥᗩ

A charcoal egg
inlaid with pearls
has a nasty surprise
for you.

Or an ivory egg
beset with onyx
will pop, shock
and vex you.

Perhaps an iridescent puzzle-box
will nix your precept paradox.

As I get stronger,
So does the illusion.
Hatch light on this
Newfangled confusion.

Is curiosity
an emotion?
Let's make it one.

Lift a stiff twig,
Climb the gold-leafed stair,
Twist chipped whitewashed shudders
And breathe a musky hall of air.

The world is a grand masterpiece
stained with our murky personages
in bizarre watercolor.

And who is the Artist?
Well, that you already know.

There I am—
a Western ascendant,
a sinister agent
in the forces of light
and pulses of right.

Dive into the spiky, spicy mirror of life,
Really sink into the black and white,
Grab the message,
The trophy,
That lofty prize,
and bolt for your life.

The mirror is closing,
And you could be sealed inside
in silence.

ꝏ

Light. Stand. Fix.

Breathe. Drink. Evolve,
with a flourish.

Think. Equate. Solve.
To be Truth
in an industry full of lies.

ᗡᗡ

Come, fluid dewdrop,
Raise the shade,
Draw the curtain,
Let light into the workshop.

Spin rosehip cantrips
on the mantle dripping with tallow and tainted water.

There are many mysteries of the deep
Humanity has yet to uncover.

I never discover,
So why search?
A grim performer
On a lacquered perch.

I never should have set that broken lens
into my eye. I was met with resistance
at the corporeal gates of heaven.

ᗡᗡ

Wanderer of ways,
Show me the wayfarer,
Glance at the stare.

Anise, my niece,
What is your chief belief?

Is it copper lorgnettes on falsetto shadows,

Swiftly on a stair of glowing tremolo?
Spread wide the French windows,
And cross where the chasm is narrow.

ᴆᴆ

Affix your eyes upon the stars,
Sharp dirty meddling scribble scribe.
Woefully unprepared, but a scholarly fellow,
Hunting a maple vial in the mishmashed marsh
mallow.

He strummed out worlds
Of sound feel and visual flavor,
as I stumbled over my bumbling manifesto.

Then blue raspberries
turn to brown palm ash,
From nightmare to daydream
and back in a flash.

Jack this journal,
Get the syrup,
Jet out of here

Before you sublimate like a cigarette
Through your soundproof cage.

Whet your wit
Before you jump
into the portal pit.

Would be a delight
If humans spun silk.
A miraculous material,
But we have our quilts.

But, do you have half a mind?
Bring that fantasy to reality,
Nation of resignation
Becomes nation of hallucination.
What is reality but the tapestry of my hallucinations?

Map. Sail. Chest.
Waiting for a new sense
and the next dimension to come down the pipes.

Idea. Pen. Permanence.
Art is the clearest mirror of life,
Lucid long after the curtain calls.
That piece of art will not move
until this city falls.

A temptress swishes her vermilion shawl,
There is something shiny upon the sprawl.

Maple enters your soul like prayers enter Yah.
Shady deals distend.
The sun is rising again.

ꝏ

What's that?
That's not typically there,
Casting a huge shadow on the Zen garden
Behind the marble mansion.

I enrobe my optical dagger
Upon a half-cloaked moondust stair,
Parting the blue jacaranda veil
To ribbon routes in air.

I bust in like black wind,
Serving a tender, juicy poem.

Swaggering lass in the sunglass,
Board the fiberglass,
And let the joke
recede into the past.

A man is his expression,
Express your experience
Like an ignited stream of gas.

ᘓᘔ

Elephants birth elephants.
Petra, rose-red rock like fingerpaint under One hand.
Winds of the deep mix quicksand,
I confront them in bowers of treetop land.

The right fiber,
In the wrong filament.
A purest florist
Bouquets from his element.

Just a moment of recreation
In elations of phytoncides and synthesis,
Dispelling majestic mystics
With the ace of creation.

ᘓᘔ

Shed like a snake in the black tool shed.
Bring dreams to bear on the light they share.
They will permeate the sugary, spearmint air
Only ever for tonight.

Even kings can fold,
This joint's gone cold.

Come, see the roses in the curtain.
Some will fare a carnation-laced stair,
But hug your medium,

Nighttime is uncertain.

ꝏ

Driftwood in the street,
Jetsam in the trees.
I deserve a moment's peace
Of tranquility.

When I'm snoring snoozing boring
Don't disturb I'm quite awake,
Most awake at four in the morning
When I'm a dreaming dopey ordeal
I'm actually all lava-eyes, exploring.

So pound the mortar to the pestle,
Measure out the water,
Sizzle on the kettle.

Pop your fun-box. Chew the leash. Kiss your captor.
Fulsome flavor, clearing smoke & a little genie for
your lamp.

ꝏ

Have you seen a man in a tuxedo?

ꝏ

Hallucinate a joint and light it up.
The senses are at your command.
From memory you may lay me a feast,
There is always an apple at hand.

Blood orange, grenadine grenade
of vision flavor eye candy,
Whipped forth by indigo
and white sandy leads,
To brave the least.

ꝏ

If you fill your days with music and poetry,

Strange and beautiful things will happen.

Every individual is significant and every nation great.

Take up your Montblanc,
Snap wide venetians,
Let light seep into this dank humidor.
Defying sin is power
Flowing through a dark corridor.

A Little Secret

River living,
Early surrealism.

I hope your illusion holds water.

Childhood as Eden,
Hypnotism. Religion. Allure.

Endearing malcontentment,
She sunk her teeth into my idea.
It's not in the rock's nature to fly.

∞

A little secret longing to be told
and ruined.
Brought to a cold
smolder.

A secret.
Don't worry about it.
It doesn't concern you
while it discerns you,
While it sweeps over you,
While it eats you.
While it is you.

Just a little secret
Smoky,
Hungry mandibles
rattling beyond the decibels.

Eye like a lash,
Mind like a cat-o'-nine.

What, what, what
do you think you see?

Eyes in the stomata.

Secret.

Translation—
Go, go, go on,
get out of here!

White Ink's Worthless

A good man is never alone.
Better in here,
than out in the arresting cold.

I feel neurons moving the eye,
have begun to dream
of dugongs.

Damn diadem of dumb Elysium,
In a vial somewhere between the worlds
of poetry & science.

Egyptian dunbeks.
Wary of this turkey,
I love the feel of this machine.
Gunpowder is extremely volatile,
A bow & arrow is so different from a gun.
This man is a machine of beats.

What's your superpower?
Who's your future father?
Howdy beastie,
Get on the big baguette.

Shepherd of sharks.
Chocolate attaché,
black jetpack.

The album moves through the art.

Dark passengers,
Candid cameras
& no closure.

Money shot—
Encounter a species,
Capture
& tame it.

I would love to go to the land of unicorns,
Please show me the way.

Will I ever find an *Ajna*
wide as my own?

Still frigid
where city melds into night.

Let's hook
is the phrase murmured by her eye.

But like marmalade on granite at night,
Want to do it right—
Spread this crumpet into life.

Biomechanics

His room is the cockpit of a music airplane.
On a plush velour couch,
The Dead fell like rain.

This beat was like an extend-o-punch,
Hooking out of the speaker.

An Old Soldier

A diamond is a legend,
but not the gem of this lesson.

One coin is a year of meals,
A fresh set of wheels.
One bar could buy a brownstone
in the heart of New York City.

The metal is mine, of course,
however it was stolen, taken by force.

Luckily, juice from the Tree
is satisfying me.

But under tundra of memory,
Truth calcifies in the cold—

Never, ever fold
from even a grain
of true gold.

My Mycologist

Solitary sandpipers and a roseate tern
crowd the estuaries of my eyes.

Every day is a treat,
Stimulation of the senses
in new rhythmic ways.

Every river crawls toward the source.
This game has run its course.

Vibrating air and captured color
are to the virtuoso blood and brother.

It's worth any cost
to break into a fresh realm of color.
The evening is an illustration
and we are diamond miners.

ထ

Hello,
Do you speak my language?
No?
Oh, I'd hoped so.

I could kiss
this mycologist,
my mycologist.
He is a sweet ivy twister.

ထ

Each of my poems is a little girl,
Before she is brushed, dry
and curled for the world.

Each of my poems is a little girl,

Before she is robbed of innocence,
and made into a whore of the world.

Pretty poem, little girl,
My fair lady of the world—
Get on a ship,
and sail like a bird.

ᗡᗡ

There will be seas of blood.
Period. End of sentence.

There is no hiding, running
from blood.

Only fear, and the eventual
warm embrace.

God damn it!
My mycologist was arrested.
They came after him with daggers & dachshunds.

Fortunately, he is of the prestige to have a protégé.

An angel with a hot sword
that can cut bone like butter
rushes through a final door
to the very end of the last corridor,

Then purest white light
with a glow of purple.

The Bad Batch

Pause to your peril,
Hesitate to your decimation.
Right this way into vivid hallucination.

Tighten your two-leathers.
Pick yourself up by the bootstraps.
Are your laces loose,
or tight on track?

There's no hiding behind those eyes.
Understand I am here fire.

Don't mount this ship.
There have been a lot
of blue skies in my life,
but none tonight.

A girl with a grisly reputation.
The backslide is our favorite pastime.

A repertoire of the salty illusory.
My hair is coming in from
the direction of the future.

A lady with an unsavory reputation.
Sushi off a female.

ᴏᴏ

Off to meet a bird.
Off to be a bird.

A bum examining an outboard motor,
A fresh plate of almond cookies.
Strange wavelengths at Waverly Place.

Not the scent I'm sniffing for.

The yippin' pup.
Surrey, Cornwall.
Chicago Minor.

Scarlet skies, flavor scryers,
Taste alchemist. Bottled magic.

Toon world.
People get comfy quickly in a castle.
Sorry if I'm slightly worse for the wear.

I spat blue phlegm—
This is the future.

Yet I will sleep on stone and pay for it
five minutes later.

Grove closure.
You in the scarlet shirt coming down the passage!

Sow your wild oatmeal.
Incubus, succubus,
move a stitch.
Inksplotched and paint-stained.

Fancy seeing you here, my dear.
Did a bad cap fall in tonight's batch?

Sniggering, sniveling,
Ensnared in and
Enfettered in a booby trap.

The escape hatch,
The bad batch,
The snickerin', snoozin' snatch.

Ink is blood.
This pen is dead,
Blasting forth in a psychedelic armoire
to the coffiny afterlife.

∞

Loose in the coiling moist.
Coil into memory,
you coy little horror.

This is an angry Tim Burton character,
This is a random encounter
in a final fantasy.

Suddenly dusky, drowsy poetry.
On bread alone on the low road,
Or honing spirit on the high?

Just an afternoon to study Japanese.
Need a light? Allow me,
for I am a man of poetry.

At the earliest gentlemanly opportunity,
Teashades and a Tam o' Shanter.
Fungus on the loamy ground.

I was blind,
but now I see.
Tomorrow fills my eye.

∞

Significant reflex,
Poetic aesthetic.

The desired effect
among late Sunday murmurs of the saloon.

Violet velvet gave us the butcher's hook.
Pit of snakes and scorpions, lion's den.

It rhymes so it must be true.
It makes no sense, that's why it's art.
My door is a portal to fresh perspective,
Just don't trip in the jagged mirror.

Why don't I set my time on fire?
Put me through trial by ordeal.

Remember when you're taut on the rack,
in the jaws of a black vise
or sealed in an iron maiden,
You have been a heathen.
And your only turn is hesed's redemption.

Nation of hallucination emerges
from the glossy chrysalis at last,
Spreading the graceful wings
of a nation of emanation.

Telegraph

Decoding the past out a spindial
in shakes of the sandglass,

I don't need to do a bit
bogged with STOP,
grossly obtuse
—though I had one prepared.
You already know.

I just need you to flick
your finger along where
dust collects in the grain
of that dated tech, your brain.

Oral redaction is gone now.
Is it loss of ability, I wonder,
or experience worth redacting?

Typesetting typographist,
Thrilled by my own madness.
What happened to our memory?

A comma to conceal the damages.
We are taught to hunt for info in the void,
to find faces in the vista.

Papyrus. Parchment. Paper.

Internet.

Is it
an empty net?

This store has every form,
Alas, you must provide first matter.
Teetering shelves of a million media
for even a novice redactor.

They have every way in the world of expression,
But it's resting on you to build up through them,
So speak with precision.

What is medium?
All, of course.

Sure, times change like a crook.
What am I going to do about that notebook?
has become keep your pad out of the drizzle.

Texting is
stars & tamales
coming down the pipes.

By the way,
it had something to do with how telegraphs
chugged the flow of information from a slow STOP.

∞

Technology tries to usurp color,
and fails.
Technology copies color,
and prevails.

Yet the true aesthetic remains, all but futile,
in a palm of the masterful beholder,
Wherever he waits in patience for a pupil.

After all,
A master just needs a spark.

The mind is the final frontier.
Timespace, a thin veneer.

The Present

Speech solidifies,
Substantiates experience.

Take a peek in my bottle.
Mixing bright
mystic quicksand,
Ink all over my hand.

Imagine away the famine.
My dusk is melted
by a cloud blue arpeggiator.

Snakes and gators
as I'm tracking a harp.
The window is bare
in my lucid nightmare.
I wrote it on the cloud.

Glass violin,
Vassal of evil,
Listen to my miracles—
Music flows like a rainbow of water out a silver
faucet.

Download a pill,
Big plans are in synthesis.

Time is a gift,
Your presence a present.
There is no gift
as great as the present.

What, you think the world a happy accident?

Every experience is a gift.
And life, the grandest gift of all.

Write a letter spirit beings can eat.
Power in every word,
In every rune there is heat.

Defecting Affectation

You write smaller toward the end of the page?
Funny, for that is where you should scream
each and every precious word.

Roll up a newspaper
and smoke ink.

Have a glass
of Gasoline.

Slip the next clip
of Dunhills in your gun,
and smack the action.

Stick your next fag
in the gas tank,
and hit the ignition.

False visual cognates,
Light inflections.

A leaf lilts
onto an old auto.
Bright little birthday candles
left on a wet black iron picnic table.
A severed ringneck wing on empty sidewalk.

Why does this playlist always run backward?

Ever expected to bite into a blood-drippy,
juicy steak,
and had your teeth hit napkins and flatware?
Nothing like a little adrenaline

to set things in perspective.
Or maybe you just popped in a chip,
and tasted your motherboard, double-dipped.

Most basically,
I placed pastels and poetry in a centrifuge,
and lavascript waltzed out.
Then I poured lyrics and graphite in a blender,
and sampled the slush of success.

Who was here just now?
Where, per se,
did I leave my black beret?
Perhaps under the birdcage.

Wait! That seat is booby-trapped
with a whoopee cushion.
Something is very funny and off
about this one slap on a digital conga.
Bastard's took my ink, iron & oil.

꘍

Something is wrong with this train.

Have you ever ascended to higher elms
with your bronze statue intact,
Or did your corpse rot and smell?

Stop treating your hovel
like a hovel,
Wild caged animal.
Who's to blame for your shuffle shame?
A woodwose, wormwood
and plain pain.

You can cage an animal,

but you'll yet wash its waste.

The bride pulls the fire alarm.
Brain scoured, mind polished,
Upgraded, empowered,
Glowered in garnish.

Sun dries sundries
mysterious & powerful.
A popcorn machine isn't that unnatural.

That bread is offal.
Life can be shameful. Uncaring, unaware.
You tumble face-first down the apples & pears.

Where will you be
when expectations
won't greet reality?

What about when you reach
for your next frosty beer
and clutch at nothing but sandy air,

Or receive a moldy banana peel
in the warm bag of your last meal?

ꝏ

I take only what I need
and not a puff more.
Why, only from time to time,
For the flavor and the feel.

Taste and feel,
Experience tastes,
But know their place.

Feckless puppet in malicious fleece
of raspberry aether droplets of time.
Concupiscent tableau of aftergames.

I'll scrape my
life off the floor
tomorrow, I promise.

He smoked a thousand
before appreciating one.

A little tickle at the back of your mind?
He must eat the talking dove.

I love the sea,
but not as much as
I fucking love taffy.

They are distortions distorted from purity,
but for one purpose alone—
To meet the Maker.
Waves

Just like me,
Where 2 cultures,
2 cubists
are to meet.

Quick by foot,
Fast by machine,
Slow by dream.

To where? Nowhere,
it is all about the glide.

∞

Things are coming in a little clearer than before.
If Lautrec's legs were any longer,
Who's to say he'd been a painter?

As for me,
If I hadn't been stone alone all these years,
I'd naught have known a verse's pulleys & gears.

Trapdoor, innkeeper—
Seven dirt short.
Why linger when the instinct
is to jet?
Shake fate with an about face
in your step.

Method of Locomotion

My face needs a path for flame to vent upward
As I'm often torching things forward
Toward the next coral chord, the lost last world.

Learn to paint.
Study your codices,
Mercy.

Maybe
Perhaps
Perception.

An engine is where
power converts to motion.

Language is where
matter meets air.

Build a world on a fruit.
There is a vision I am trying to realize,
But it requires so much order.
Sometimes these spots of dark color
drag me to the lowest circle.

How to bring Hebrew into English...
Take a late pattern and squash it.

Where does concept become symbol?
Do we deign to put thought into words?
We deign,
but avail?
Maybe.

A sign
to continue on
to the next page.

Where sound meets motion,
Where dreams set the quotient,
When signs divulge their potency—
A golden locomotive begins its engine.
ᘓᘔ
Where do good and evil gather together?
That is called
Humor.

I put the hell in
Hello,
Do you speak my language?
No, didn't think so.

It smells like you're up to something.
At the mere sight of Zeppelin,
weak bands cower.

Alas, where do dreams end
and life begin?

With the clink, gear and purr
of metal. Loud, clanking,
rarely precious,
Metal is the mechanism
of dreams meeting life.

We take the plunge,
like driving the carriage off the dock
straight into watery kingdom,
where it's sipped into the hegemony fold

after its dying gasp.
That fearsome incredible crash
of tons of twisted metal
meeting the innocent sea,
And then that final gurgle of the sea's poetic victory.

                ᴆᴆ

Language is the purest mirror of a people.
We communicate
via air, light and fate.

Art is the sharpest mirror of life,
Although language can be a delight,
Language is the sad mirror of our spite.

Basquiat squeaked truth,
Language is a living beast
and she is not pleased.

Language is alive—
Hugs, bites and kicks
Like a wild bull at times,
but it *is* us,
the lifelong defined.

Sword Ink Flower

Always a sword, never a friend.
Sometimes a sword is your only friend.

To say nothing of the pen.
To say nothing with your pen?
Well, verse.

A verse would be nice.
A hearse would be nice.
Thirsty from rice,
accursed by the dice.

God will let me pursue my vision—
Bring color into the mix,
a red pen and a black one switch.
This is the now, friends,
Live.

That will be the time,
This will be the poem
Where Yah, sweet Yah
Will pursue my vision.

Kettle Portal Vehicle

White, black or green teas?
I could drink one of these,
to slake this thirsty snail.

I don't need quite much,
Just twelve silver cylinders
& a dash of teak gauges.

I tune my vernacular,
Polish my expression
and tap my metronome to the floor.

Ancient Japanese Mounts

It is a new day.
Turn the lamp.

God created the guitarist,
the guitar,
and strummed.

We are his precious vicarious vessels
of sense and experience.

There is a land far east of the Jordan,
to where I must now go.

ಹ

Signs.
She will only hurt you in the end.
Extensive use of Prussian Blue.

Hungry steel just went to the dentist.

Whipchains and beartraps,
Fetters and snares.

Scorpion, scorpion.

You in the
bottom of the chasm,
Leap for your life—
You have the kind of *koaḥ* that changes fates.

An inexorable wave of disconcertion,
ten times Fundy at high tide
on my low-lying valley weald.

A Haligonian aquacaust
reminds only the past can be lost.
Now, a step in the light direction,
To a different yield.

Stone Rose Stair

My name twiddles
on lips of the flute.

My walking magnolias
stoop & take root.

This watch will stop long after
my heart is a drop in the ground.

I near the palace
as lights convolute.

A stone stair wraps around
the back, strewn with roses.

One-eyed Jack

Draft an improv,
Vintage a symphony.

I love when magicians
meld from the mist.

This game is pure poetry.
"An empty canvas holds infinite possibilities."

Splash black
& end the shit.

I am a wicked magic player,
Dying for a duel.

My ink lives and breathes.

In years, a child.
In vision, an elder.

Bayou

The light is white and green
in playful exchange with shadow
in the scrubland of this lysergic dream.
Neural gnats cling to the screen.

With no further ado,
Not a thing between
me and the dew of this dream,
I become a gnat in the bayou.

A plant is a village,
A tree a town,
A cactus, a fortress,
& wind the only sound.

A plant is a village of white & green,
Wind washes the scrubland and bayou clean.

Summer by South
FOR ROBYN WEINER

I wander where they are,
Could they be doves in air?

Flooding bright influx
of bronze light flexuous
& curvaceous,
Outlining the burning chimera
beyond the retina.

I would love to rub our essences together
as it is snowing underwater,
Form an enclave in the mossy rock.

Hey robin, how was your flight
Through isoparaffin & camphor night?

Now you stand before me
Replete with garden and grove,
Where I forge you fluid letters
in air and heat.

Will you cry in fright or delight
when I approach from behind
on a shaded boulevard?

Will you hiss from the mast
as a ghostly schooner,
When I edge nearer
your pleasure-center?

Signs in the sky turning rose
dance through a font of living jewels,

linger on prismatic skin
of my robin in repose.

The way you wish us tonight
is my greatest voyage,
It's been a cold year since you left the nest.

Yeah, a sharp minute.
Our last lunch was a hot second
of open flames & genitalia,
We crunched munchy crisp romaine
as our time was vivisected
and sectioned, gone in a wisp
of skeleton and skin.

ᗡᗡ

Peach fruit on a silver platter,
Her eyes are vials of grade-A dark amber.

In the unfriendly parataxia
of carrion comfort darksome devouring,
I eat bread and peaches.

From simple and quiet
to loud and complex emotive thoughts
digressing the mindset.

Reupholster me into the upholstery,
There is nothing greater
than bringing a life into this world.

ᗡᗡ

A Tibetan shawl in jade
is just the ticket for my robin.

A blue summer rose,
My sweet robin in repose.

Every eyelash a grain of gold,
The very skin topaz aglow.

∞

Desperate for a drink
in a dangerous elevator.
Swept again by her wave and camber,
Drizzled in the grade-A dark amber.

With a whirlwind of a mind like mine,
This is what is when I think of you.

There's ice in the desert,
Fire on the glacier.
King-size dove down one day,
milky thunder.

Sit sweetly and sugar your tea.
The robin is close at hand.

Where you have struggled,
you will prosper.
Time laps up bark of the poplar.

One day she will blossom before me.

Let my smile suck you in lemon-limes.
I'm last on your mind as you're first on mine.

What she'll wear tonight
is of greater import
than my life's work.

What she may grace me in tonight
trumps my every ace, flower & play of light.

North by Death

A sharp cat,
A smooth cat,
Black cat round.
Violin spider.

Doves—
There is no comparison.
There is no comparison to my dove.

She rushes past in a blast of perfumed air.

The link between man and dove is a complex,
beautiful one,
which flushes out the vast masterpiece that is the
world.

Do we exist inside of them,
Are they in our gust? What if people
looked like doves, and doves
like us? Would we, dove-people,
be capable of love?
                        ᴐᴆ
This morning my dove brought me
a poem tasseled to her leg.

Grumble and groan on your Jack Jones.
Wipe the smug from your gulp & glug.
Someone dovenapped her, twice.
Both times, she waited on the fence across the way.

My dove in an inglewood,
Brambles of the viscera.

It might be up to you
when the time arrives,
To lead him down the right path.

Let him be,
Set him free,
So he may glide like a rainbow
to the dyads of a zebra finch.

I'm going to fly off
this rock, yes I
Will. Tonight
I fly, tonight
I FLY

Take up a chopstick,
See the sunflowers
in rice paper blinds.
A scent of cherry wood.

Do you know doves yawn,
Do you know they kiss?
Fly into my life
& migrate away, tenebrist.

I could hear patters of wings no more—
My deft dove left lying on the floor.

My bird cannot chirp
while it sleeps.

My dove died today,
I cannot imagine a greater pain.
Why does the Lord give
and snap away?

To feel the brown bread dove in hand
cold and lifeless like that
was pure agony.

Limp unresponsive
From fervent exchange,
A swift end to the allegory.

Cause of death—
Unknown.

I lost her and my white mountains.

Dry your tears,
The Lord is here.

Gone

This can go ahead and end

There was a time when I cared

That time has passed

There was an age when I loved

It was long ago

There were years when I felt

What I no longer feel now

I am torn

From the life I once led

My thoughts and emotions

Have bled out

And there is no more

To be said

Wet Red Words

Sam's maple cake.
There is no comparison
to Harrison.

Stand on the X.
Rip and dip. Burn and bounce.
Green headlights

California nonsense
Turret shadow curb appeal,
Upshot of a snapshot snapped shut.

drain the horn

poison garden castle town floating world
prussic acid

Interstellar medium.
Quick jellyfish, waffles on the roof.
Roof waffle,
Maple of my eye—
Whoa that woman at 2boots was crazy haggard
and snaggletoothed.

In fjord, Dunhills to dunghills.

Brace my tonfa
In an alternate Yamato.
One day I'll tea in Edo's tea gardens.
I wish I was a black ship.

Ancient Japanese mounts.
You are a wet candy wrapper
At midnight sundeck powwows.

70

Strike while the iron is hot.
A new broom sweeps clean.
Technique is the tradition.

Syllepsis eggcorn mondegreen
Scribomanic graphorrhea,
I Want to be the Guy.

Can I get a little symbiosis
to my countertoppy goodness?
Grand gland.

Libretto cantada,
the air is like blankets.
Breviloquence succinct to
Magniloquence. Ardent horny dispassionate
Clairgustance.

城下町- *jōkamachi* -Japanese palace town

Sail into her port,
Stick my Cairo in her genizah.
It is a small miracle that I am here.

I had a dream that I fell in the tracks,
it didn't end sweetly.

Grgh, look formidable... glowstick.
Headsmoke.

80

From sensei to *seito*,
Disciple to guru.

Enfilading,

Crack the earth in half like a jawbreaker,
Saw the earth in half like a cherry-filled truffle.

The weight of my ideas leaden the page.
Oil underwater rushes over circuit breakers.

Extrapolate
Ignominious
Brood of vipers...
Drink the words of the wise with eagerness.

I am the professional poet
With a life full of collectible crap.
You can't bottle my magic and sell it on Broadway.

Rock will set you free.

A smoldering gaze for the dust mite
On my needle.

Redirect tellurian time to heavenly ideals.
Be a voice of light and reason among creation.

90

Gummy buddha.
What if we were sticks of gum,

Chewed and gray in the gutter?

The way concrete cuts light completely.
Akiva at Insalai,
Apply fire.

Shirts are for chumps,
the same chumps who get haircuts.
Same for jobs, wives and normal lives.

Rainbow striking adze,
I've seen things that'd make you a ghost.
Velvet violet *mefo'eret.*

I approve of you whatever you do, rabbi.

The raven in the craven,
The word in the sword,
A storm of a man.

Gemara on the beach,
Pocket dial the band.
Stop researching cocktails and come over here.

Smoke in a bottle,
Spill his soul into her body.

Slam puppetry.

Avifauna. Neighborhood decay.
Railroad vine, dune panic grass.

Whimbrels. Orioles
out a fishbowl

Errata zebra,
Candelabra, brassiere.
Venomous denouement.

A bit scanter
than it was.

Husks.
I almost
Threw my pen off the sundeck,
a fountain of missile at 200 feet.

100

Follow me to an eternity
of tawdry music and poetry.

Lunar drive,
Solar piston.

Trotsky.
Cotton gin.
The Battle of the Bulge.

When confronted in regard to Steven's azury guitar
irregular, covertly starry, I wink & whisper
The Truth is in the poem.
ထ
You do realize the only rhyme is Jeroboam.
Truly, eternally, seemingly tawdrily,
"Poetry is the subject of the poem."

Seaside to cityside.
I cared for you a great deal,
Now I'm just trying to forget.

Forgive the dated parlance,
You have a Chinaman's chance.

Reset emulation—
My dove is that last plug of gum,
The lucky cigarette,
Somehow the tastiest thing ever.

El Significado de los Sueños

Monday is a sturgeon
in watery grasp of the great jar.

An eye in a palm will sweep it to
air.

Lust

A hand that always seeks
a soft pink underbelly.

Why is the hand of need
forever in plea?

Does it grasp? It surely sees
right through, transparently.

But how and why
does a hand need sight to get by?

Evolution is getting carried away.
How can the very pores and finger nerves
headache for lust yet silt with sawdust?

Sight washes the way white,
but desire clouds the road again with
angry red dirt.

Hot Road

Hot road, come home.
Hot road all alone.

Freight train, frame of lead,
Late train, I'm brown bread.
Freight train, full steam ahead.

Your cola's warm
and your lover's cold,
I settle in the storms
I used to know.

Hot road, red iron dust,
Point me home before I rust.

Chilly street really needs
a little, sweet seed
blooming into you next to me.

Ova

What alchemy on the alebench
caused this sweet ornament of life?
The vicious circle of the wench
becomes the sweet cycle of light.

The absonant are abstracted
in the bright alpine round,
Then accosted and abated
by the ballasting bagpipe sound
Heralding a new ornament of life
at noon of night.

All's Quiet on the West End

All's quiet on the west end.
All's smooth on the east end.
Truth is,
Beginners never know their friends.

All's quiet uptown,
All's smooth downtown.
Truth is,
Clowns can also frown.

Everything when I met you
became my refuge.
This is
A cataclysmic tune.

Tanned in the beach sun,
Standing under beech nuts.
This is
Not mnemonic much.

As it is such,
It is wont to seem,
Once more and for the last
Sparkling fiend in the delta lusty.

All's quiet on the west end,
All's smooth on the east end.
Truth is,
I've never made amends.

All's quiet uptown,
All's smooth downtown.
Truth is,

I'm no proper noun.

Same as when I met you
I have no refuge.
This is
Coming to a fuse.

Fanned by palm fronds,
Queen of automatons,
If this is it, it's just wrong—
Lily and ash in the same pond.

腐敗と再生

雷茶

私は縛ら

竜です

Rot & Renewal

Lightning. Tea.

I am a tied

dragon.

שוקע

אתה גשם עלי

אני צמא ורעב
כאשר בגן פגשת אותי

אויר חם נושב
האוירה אחרי חורפי

יש חם אחד לדם
אני זוכר שפעם
דם וחלב היו כל דבר

אני לא יכול לשכוח שהעולם
עוד שוקע במדבר

Sinking

You are rain upon me.

I am thirsty and ravenous
When you encounter me in the garden.

Warm air blows.
The atmosphere is beyond wintry.

There is a singular warmth to blood.
I remember that once,
Blood and milk were everything.

I am not able to forget that the world
Is still sinking in the desert.

A Door Opens

Vanity of vanities.
A door opens.

You fly down the halls
much quicker this year.

The rusted gate
has spread at length.

The last glass stair appears.
You part the final gossamer veil

to reveal light,
and a profounder bliss.